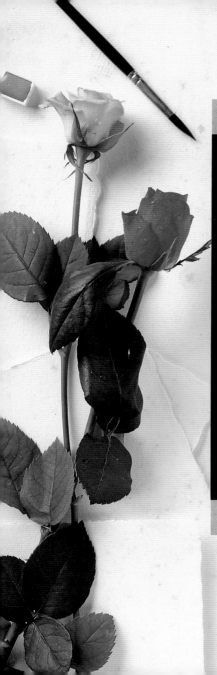

THE
WATERCOLOUR
FLOWER
PAINTER'S
POCKET PALETTE

Instant visual reference on
colours and shapes

Elisabeth Harden

B T Batsford Limited, London

THE FLOWER COLOURS

First published in
Great Britain by
B T Batsford Limited,
London
4 Fitzhardinge Street,
London W1H 0AH

Copyright © 1996
Quarto Publishing
plc.

ISBN 0-7134-7948-5

A catalogue record
for this book is
available from the
British Library

This book was
designed and
produced by
Quarto Publishing
plc.
The Old Brewery
6 Blundell Street
London N7 9BH

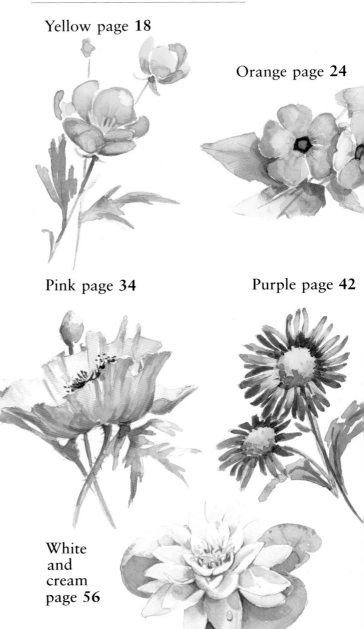

CONTENTS

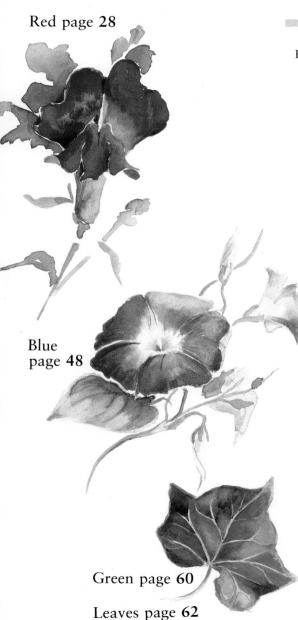

Red page 28

Blue
page 48

Green page 60

Leaves page 62

HOW TO USE THIS BOOK

THE AIM OF this book is to offer a series of step-by-step flower portraits which explain the techniques involved, and analyze the particular colour mixes required to create a spectrum of flower shades ranging from cool whites to richest purples.

The flowers are categorized into a series of basic shapes. An introduction describes each type, and the drawings examine the perspective and patterns of light and shadow that make up the three-dimensional form.

This colour code indicates a selection of flowers in a particular colour range and suggests particular paint mixes required to achieve a wide variety of tone, and subtle colour variations.

Flowers are identified by their common names, and at least one example of each basic flower shape is shown. This highlights the characteristics of each.

Each flower is painted as a sequence of one or two steps and a final painting. Captions describe colours used, the colour mixes required and the techniques involved (see also pages 6–9).

Colours suggest the light-reflecting areas and the densest shadows where mixing dark but lively colours is tricky.

Obviously this is a limited selection and the general principles can be extended into your own mix-and-match system.

Most of the flowers have been painted with light falling from top right. Note your light source and build flower shape accordingly.

COLOUR FOR FLOWER PAINTERS

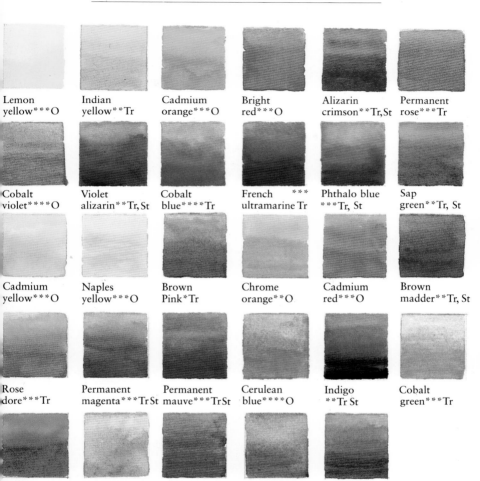

Lemon yellow***O

Indian yellow**Tr

Cadmium orange***O

Bright red***O

Alizarin crimson**Tr, St

Permanent rose***Tr

Cobalt violet****O

Violet alizarin**Tr, St

Cobalt blue****Tr

French ultramarine Tr ***

Phthalo blue ***Tr, St

Sap green**Tr, St

Cadmium yellow***O

Naples yellow***O

Brown Pink*Tr

Chrome orange**O

Cadmium red***O

Brown madder**Tr, St

Rose dore***Tr

Permanent magenta***TrSt

Permanent mauve***TrSt

Cerulean blue****O

Indigo **Tr St

Cobalt green***Tr

Phthalo green***Tr

Raw sienna ****Tr

Burnt sienna****Tr

Raw umber ****O

Burnt umber ****O

CODES

****	Extremely permanent	O	Semi-opaque colours
***	Durable colour	Tr	Transparent or semi-transparent colours
**	Moderately durable colour	St	Particularly staining colours
*	Fugitive colour		

TECHNIQUES

WATERCOLOUR PAINT CAN BE manipulated in a number of exciting ways. Some techniques are extremely valuable for flower painters and produce textures and patterns unobtainable with a paintbrush.

Always remember the basic essentials for successful painting: a well ordered work space, clean paints and plenty of clear water.

WASHES

A wash is a flat area of colour sometimes graduating to a darker shade. Mix enough paint for the whole area and apply with a good sized brush, mixing in a little water for the paler areas. Work subsequent layers quickly so as not to disturb the paint below.

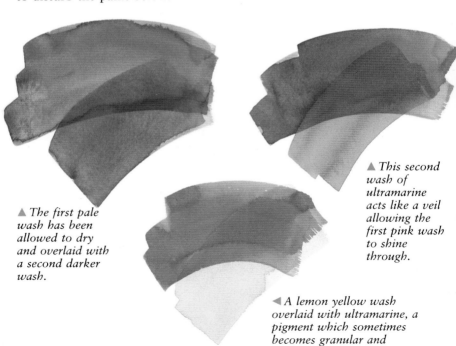

▲ *This second wash of ultramarine acts like a veil allowing the first pink wash to shine through.*

▲ *The first pale wash has been allowed to dry and overlaid with a second darker wash.*

◄ *A lemon yellow wash overlaid with ultramarine, a pigment which sometimes becomes granular and produces interesting textures.*

DRY BRUSH

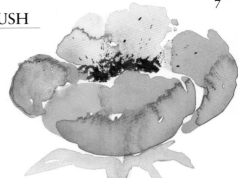

Textures and petal marking can be made with a dry brush. Spread the bristles of a square-ended brush and use a little paint to create fine lines. A stiff brush can also be used for spattering and stippling paint – for stamens or speckling.

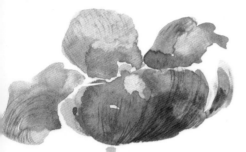

◄ *A dry brush spread between finger and thumb and dabbed in dryish paint was used to make these fine lines.*

▲ *Dark speckles made by spattering paint off a brush with thumb or knife.*

LIFTING OUT

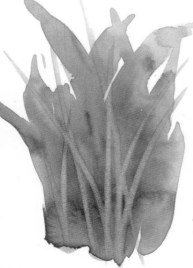

A sponge, tissue or cotton bud can lift damp paint, revealing soft highlights. To remove dry paint work clean water into the paint with a firm brush. Dab out the loose pigment.

► *These petal highlights were removed with a tissue.*
◄ *Thin lines of clean water were brushed into the paint and the colour dabbed out to create stems.*

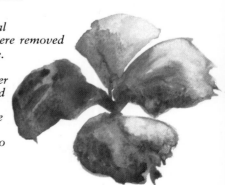

WET-ON-WET

Paint dropped onto damp paper will spread and create random patterns. More paint dropped into this will push the first paint back and dry into ruffled edges – just like petals. Feeding drier paint into a wash gives a subtle blending of colour. Both methods are unpredictable and hence magical.

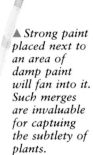

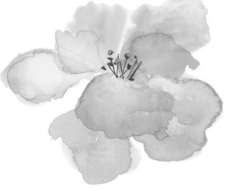

◄ Back petals: drop paint onto wet paper. Hard-edged petals: drop water into drying paint. The front petals: paint in a loose wash of yellow and drop a darker yellow paint in as it dries.

▲ Strong paint placed next to an area of damp paint will fan into it. Such merges are invaluable for captuing the subtlety of plants.

CORRECTIONS

Contrary to beginners' fears it is perfectly possible to make corrections in watercolour. Some staining pigments are difficult to remove but others wash out easily and result in subtle surprises.

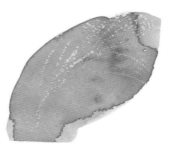

◄ Odd dots of unwanted colour can be removed with a sharp knife or scalpel. This is also a way of creating highlights.

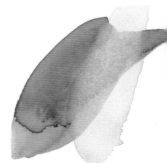

MASKING

Masking fluid can be used to block out areas from a covering wash, either retaining white or protecting a colour from a subsequent layer. Paint tends to pool around masked areas giving a greater intensity of colour and a sharp edge.

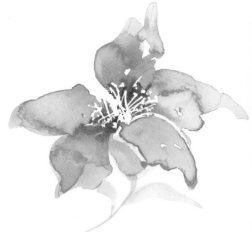

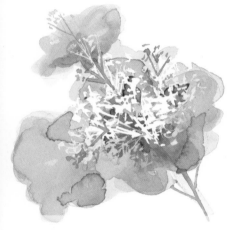

◄ *Masking fluid can be used to retain both white and coloured areas under several layers of paint.*

▲ *Masking fluid masks the stamens and is rubbed off when the wash is dry. It ruins brushes so wash them quickly.*

◄ *Washing with a soft brush will gently remove paint.*

◄ *More permanent pigments can be removed with a stiff, damp brush and tissue, though the weakened paper won't successfully take further paint.*

FLOWER SHAPES

BELLS

Bell-shaped flowers are generally seen with the light striking the upper dome and dark areas of shadow in the interior. Therefore pay particular attention to the way the stem joins the flower, its curve and colour, and the character of the stamens inside the bell – sometimes just a tiny dot, sometimes a thrusting cluster of spikes. Petal edges will be seen as very light against the dark interior and should be sharply defined. Some might be smooth and curved, others ragged and uneven. The front edge should be sharper than the back edge.

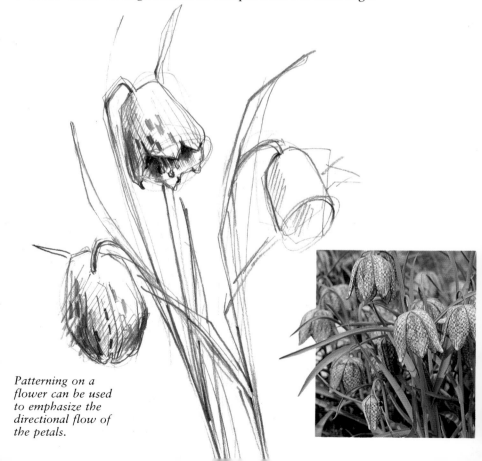

Patterning on a flower can be used to emphasize the directional flow of the petals.

TRUMPETS

A simple trumpet resembles a cone – roughly elliptical at one end and narrowing to a point. The lower edges of the tube will be in shadow, and the inside of the trumpet darker still. Make sure that the spine or centre of each petal curves into this point as it will help to indicate the flower's splaying character. Use dark tones for the inside of the trumpet where it receives no light. The stamens will indicate the tubular nature of the flower, so use very dark tones for the shadowed areas between them, and notice also the shadows they cast. More complicated trumpets include the daffodil. The principles of a simple trumpet apply.

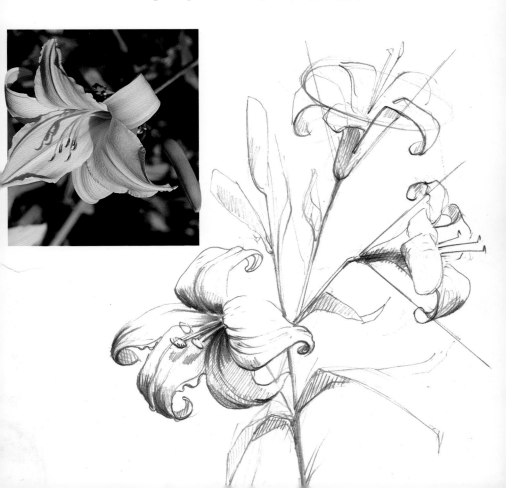

MULTIHEADED

Think of a multiheaded flower as a whole and then analyze the different components that make up this whole. In some cases it will be a tight shape like a ball with the underside of the flower head in deep shadow and upper parts partially dissolved by light. This same principle applies to multiheaded flowers of a looser nature. One of the secrets of painting a complicated multiheaded flower is to paint areas close to the eye in strong colour and sharp detail, and to make distant blossom pale and hazy.

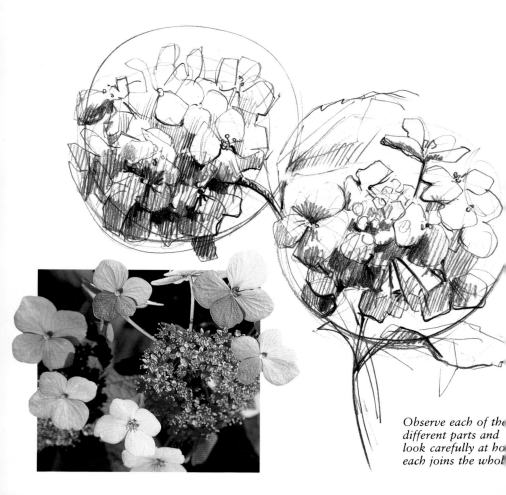

Observe each of the different parts and look carefully at how each joins the whole

SPIKES

As with pompoms, treat this flower as a whole. Think of it as a cylinder. Analyze the general pattern of light and shade that make up the overall shape by looking through half-closed eyes at the silhouette and draw this shape. Then feature the particular: look closely at each floret, its form and the shadows it casts on surrounding florets and pick out some areas in detail. Some spikes consist of a series of flower blocks and leaves set at intervals on a stem. The line of this stem becomes very important. Follow this line through the whole shape.

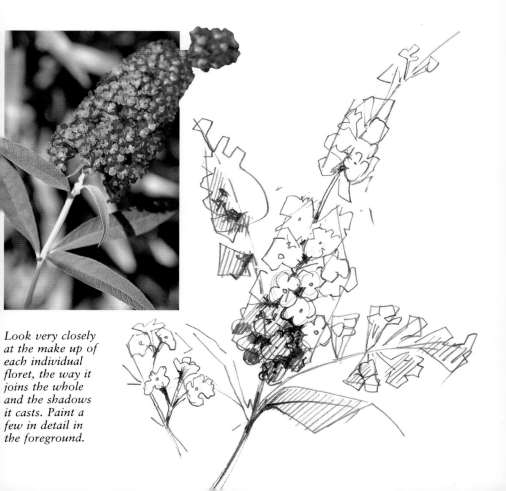

Look very closely at the make up of each individual floret, the way it joins the whole and the shadows it casts. Paint a few in detail in the foreground.

RAYS AND POMPOMS

Rays are always based on a circle – round when viewed head-on but altered by perspective to a flattened disc as the flower turns away. The central dome acts in the same way. Take careful note of how and where the stem joins the flower and the features of that junction – bulky calyx or smooth join.

Pompom shapes range from a domed circle to a globe. In each case treat the flower as a whole rather than a cluster of individual petals. Having formed the basic shape, pick out a few petals to paint in detail.

Shadows tend to occur where top petals join the dome, on the underside of this central disc, and on the lower tips of lower petals.

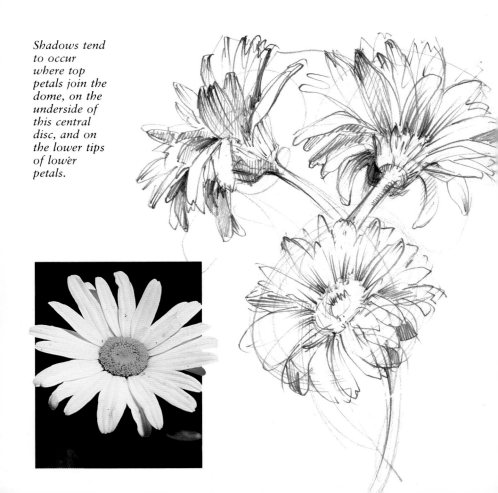

SIMPLE STARS

This is one of the easiest of types of flower to draw. Features to note are whether petals are each the same size, their texture, variation in tone and markings and the character of the edges – frilled, pointed or upturned. The flower centres are clearly visible and can range from a series of miniscule dots to an exploding burst of stamens. This, together with the grouping of flowers on the stem, as single blossoms or as a cluster, gives these flowers their identity.

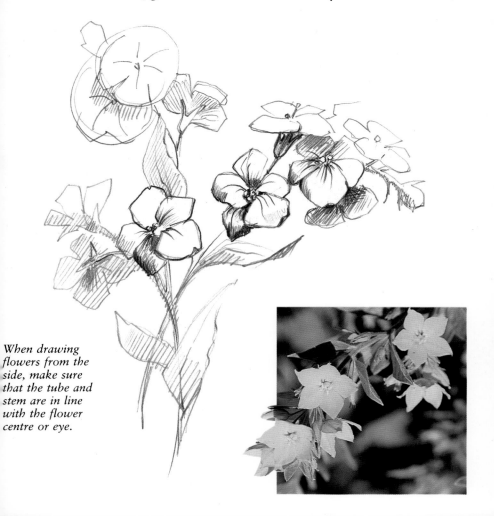

When drawing flowers from the side, make sure that the tube and stem are in line with the flower centre or eye.

LIPPED AND BEARDED FLOWERS

This type bears close examination because even the most complex flower will reveal a simple underlying pattern. When cut in half each side resembles the other exactly. When you have worked out the basic structure, then note the relative size of each petal, its texture and markings. As petals bend away from the light source and where they overlap, there will be shadows, and the centre of the flower may be very dark both in colour and tone.

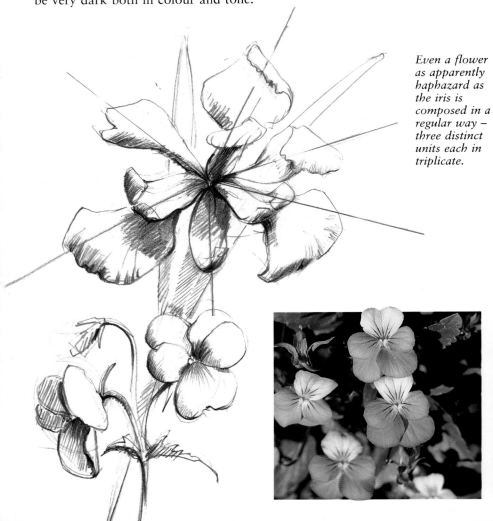

Even a flower as apparently haphazard as the iris is composed in a regular way – three distinct units each in triplicate.

CUP AND BOWL

Think of these flowers, as the names suggest, as flat bowls or deep cups. The lip of the bowl or cup seen from above is a circle, but as it turns away from the eye it becomes an elipse. Shadows are soft and delicately graduated on the upturned face of the flower, emphasizing the gentle curve of the petals, and dense and dark on the underside.

Look carefully at the way the flower head sits on the stem, the nature of this junction and the positioning of the leaves in the stem.

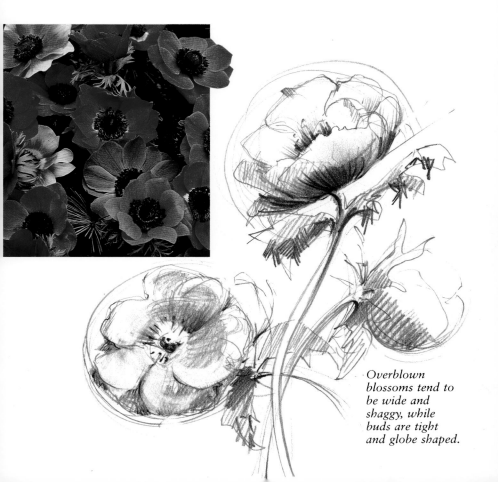

Overblown blossoms tend to be wide and shaggy, while buds are tight and globe shaped.

Yellow

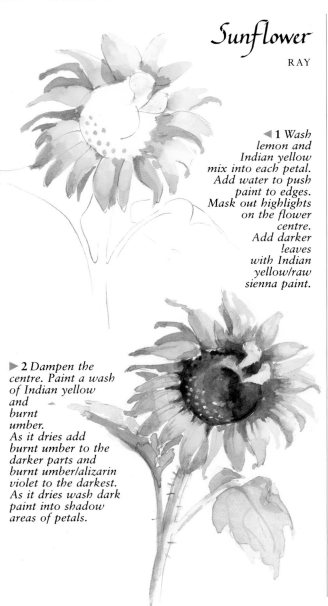

Sunflower

RAY

◀ **1** Wash lemon and Indian yellow mix into each petal. Add water to push paint to edges. Mask out highlights on the flower centre. Add darker leaves with Indian yellow/raw sienna paint.

▶ **2** Dampen the centre. Paint a wash of Indian yellow and burnt umber. As it dries add burnt umber to the darker parts and burnt umber/alizarin violet to the darkest. As it dries wash dark paint into shadow areas of petals.

1 Paint lemon yellow wash onto the petal, leaving some white highlights.

▲ **2** Build up the bell shape with cobalt green and raw umber touched into the drying paint.

Clematis

BELL

▲ **3** Paint details into the leaves with Naples yellow/raw umber mix and sap green/lemon yellow mix.

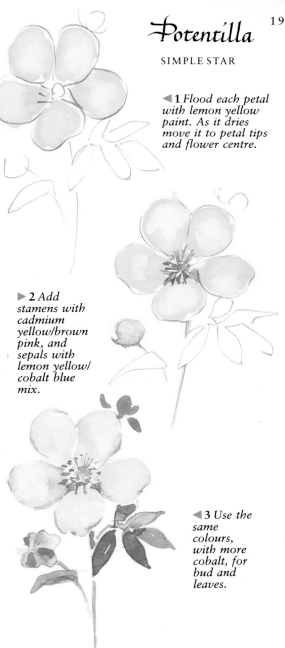

◀ 1 *Paint the flowers in various mixes of Naples yellow/lemon yellow. Drop water in to lighten upper edges of flower.*

Potentilla

SIMPLE STAR

◀ 1 *Flood each petal with lemon yellow paint. As it dries move it to petal tips and flower centre.*

Mullein

SPIKE

▶ 2 *Add stamens with cadmium yellow/brown pink, and sepals with lemon yellow/ cobalt blue mix.*

2 *Pick out stamens in brown pink. Add Naples yellow/cobalt green for shadowed petals.*

▶ 3 *Fill in the main and side stems in cobalt green. Allow it to mix occasionally with the yellow.*

◀ 3 *Use the same colours, with more cobalt, for bud and leaves.*

Yellow

Mimosa

MULTIHEADED

► **1** *Paint puddles of lemon yellow in varying strengths to show near and far flowers. Drop water into some parts to push paint to edges. Paint skeleton of spray in pale green.*

◄ **2** *Build up roundness of the nearer globes with Indian yellow and some raw sienna/sap green. Fill in leaves and stems round flowers in yellowy green.*

◄ **1** *Drop cadmium yellow and Indian yellow into the petal. Drop water in to spread the paint.*

2 *Use Indian yellow with a touch of raw umber to add petal detail. Wash out highlights on front petal.*

Iris

LIPPED

► **3** *Paint details with raw sienna. Use sap green/ raw umber mix on the stem.*

Daffodil
TRUMPET

Buttercup
BOWL

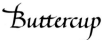

◀ **1** *Build up the petals with stripes of Indian yellow/Naples yellow mix. Leave white lines for petal ridges.*

◀ **1** *Flood Indian yellow/ lemon yellow into light-facing petals. Remove highlights as it dries.*

2 *Wash Indian yellow into the trumpet shape. Push it full strength to edges. Wash patches of chrome orange into darker areas. Use a lemon yellow/sap green wash for leaves.*

◀ **2** *Indian yellow/brown pink for undersides of petals.*

▶ **3** *Pick out petal shadows with Indian yellow/raw umber mix. For dark areas of the trumpet add touches of strong raw and burnt sienna. Emphasise strap leaves in a darker sap green.*

▶ **3** *Add cobalt blue to the mix and sharpen shadow lines. Add stamens in lemon yellow, and leaves in sap green.*

SUNFLOWERS

Betty Carr
(28" × 21")

THE RICH VIOLET of the jug and subtle lilacs of the oriental vase enhance brilliant yellow flowers. The painter has used many shades of blues and purples, and yellows ranging from lemon to deep cadmium, and has used mixes of these dark and light colours to create subtle mid-tones.

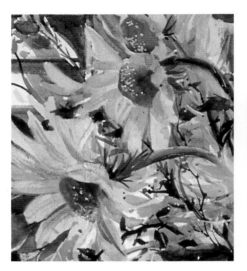

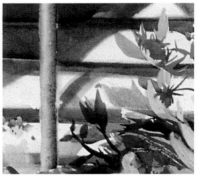

▼ The background flowers are indicated rather than painted in detail, petals with a stroke of a thick brush and a fine rigger brush used for the stem and frill of leaves.

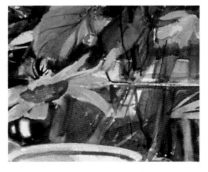

▲ Shadowed parts of flowers need particular care – the darker tones are built up by adding red and burnt sienna. For the deepest areas a touch of violet has been added to the yellow.

◄ Reflection and deflection create their own patterns. These stems have become a jigsaw of greens, deep blue and white, and stems are angled to lead the eye to the flowers above.

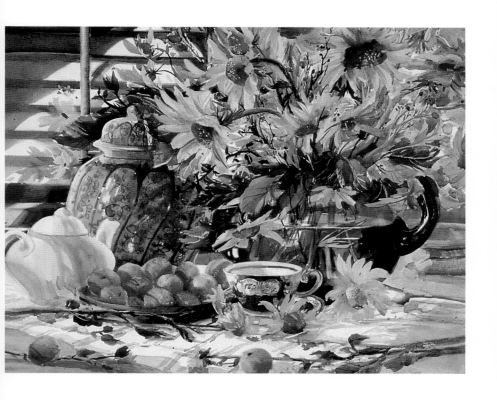

Orange

Wallflower

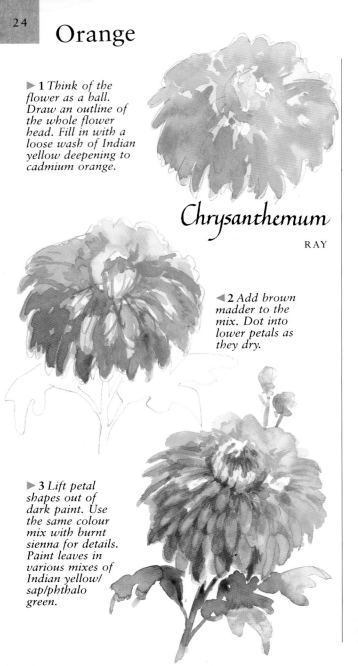

Chrysanthemum

RAY

▶ **1** *Think of the flower as a ball. Draw an outline of the whole flower head. Fill in with a loose wash of Indian yellow deepening to cadmium orange.*

◀ **2** *Add brown madder to the mix. Dot into lower petals as they dry.*

▶ **3** *Lift petal shapes out of dark paint. Use the same colour mix with burnt sienna for details. Paint leaves in various mixes of Indian yellow/ sap/phthalo green.*

▶ **1** *Paint main petals full strength Indian yellow. Allow it to create strong edges. As it dries touch raw sienna into the shadows. Same for other petals. Use a fine brush to dampen areas and lift out highlights.*

▶ **2** *Use a fine brush to paint petal markings in burnt sienna and add stalks of sap green.*

◀ **1** Paint a variegated wash of Indian yellow onto main petals and a light wash of lemon yellow onto stem and leaves. Leave some white areas.

◀ **1** Wash Indian yellow into front petals. As it dries add cadmium orange.

Strelitzia

LIPPED

2 Wash a mix of cadmium red/Indian yellow over the petals, except for white and yellow areas. Feed more paint in as it dries. Mask out stamens.

Crown imperial

BELL

▶ **3** Mix brown madder into the mix. Paint the lower petals, varying tone and shade. Add darker sap green to stem and leaves. Remove masking and paint Indian yellow stamens.

◀ **2** Fill in back petals, letting deeper cadmium orange flow into the bases. Paint the stamen ultramarine. Wash cadmium yellow/ cadmium red lightly into flower base.

▲ **3** Deepen the petal shadows. Damp the flower base and flood in phthalo green.

Orange

Red Hot poker

SPIKE

◀ **1** Paint a multitude of petals radiating from the centre. Use bright red/cadmium yellow mix for the top petal and cadmium yellow for the lower petals. Allow the colours to mix slightly and dot cadmium yellow amongst the orange.

▶ **1** Mask stamens with masking fluid and paint a variegated wash of Indian yellow, leaving white highlights. Mix in a touch of bright red for the petal bases.

2 Add more bright red and paint shadowed petals.

▶ **2** When dry use a fine, firm brush to lift paint from each floret and raw sienna/bright red mix to emphasise dark areas.

Day lily

TRUMPET

▶ **3** Use a darker mix to paint petal ridges. Add brown madder and work into the centre of the trumpet creating crisp white edges to the front petals. Remove masking fluid and paint light Indian yellow stamens.

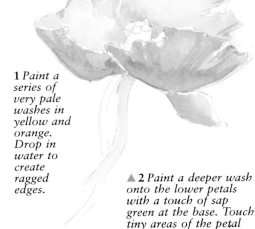

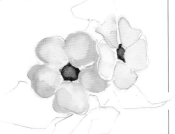

▶ **1** *Paint each petal in Indian yellow/chrome orange mix. Wash out centres to create sharp edges.*

1 *Paint a series of very pale washes in yellow and orange. Drop in water to create ragged edges.*

▲ **2** *Paint a deeper wash onto the lower petals with a touch of sap green at the base. Touch tiny areas of the petal edge with cadmium orange.*

▶ **2** *Add the black centres with an indigo/ burnt umber mix.*

Iceland poppy

BOWL

Black-eyed Susan

SIMPLE STAR

▼ **3** *Paint fine lines radiating from centres in Indian yellow. On the darker side allow the centre paint to blend in.*

▲ **3** *Deepen the lower areas. Fill in flower centre and stem with Indian yellow/sap green mix. Use very dilute paint for the shadow of the stem behind.*

Red

Bottlebrush

SPIKE

Fritillary

BELL

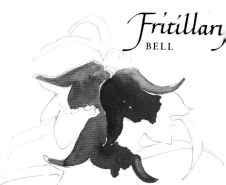

◀ 1 Use masking fluid to block out the stamen ends. Only a few will show, but they will add sparkle to the strong red. Paint the stem in a mixture of lemon yellow and sap green, allowing the two to mix.

2 Use a fine rigger brush and dryish cadmium red to create a mass of fine stamens. Build up a second, nearer layer with bright red.

▶ 3 Add depth to the areas of shadow by adding brown madder to the mix. Remove the masking fluid with an eraser.

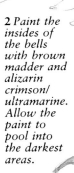

2 Paint the insides of the bells with brown madder and alizarin crimson/ ultramarine. Allow the paint to pool into the darkest areas.

▲ 1 Paint a wash of alizarin crimson on the light-facing petals of the flowers. Dab out light areas and build it up with cobalt blue and a mixture of ultramarine/ brown madder.

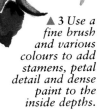

▲ 3 Use a fine brush and various colours to add stamens, petal detail and dense paint to the inside depths.

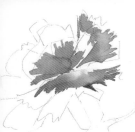

▲1 Paint a faint lemon yellow tinge on the upturned petals. Add a mix of permanent rose and bright red as a first wash. Allow the paint to pool on the lower edges.

Carnation

RAY

2 Add a mixture of alizarin crimson and bright red to the deeper petals. Tip the paper to allow the paint to settle round the spiky edges of the light petals.

Snapdragon

LIPPED

▶ 1 Damp each petal in turn. Add a hint of cobalt blue to the lower edge. Add a mixture of alizarin crimson and cobalt blue just above, followed by alizarin crimson in the top half.

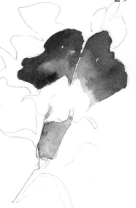

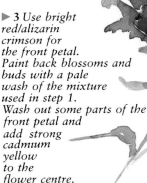

◀2 Use a touch of ultramarine to paint shadow in the second petal. Paint cobalt blue on the light side of the flower body. Use alizarin crimson and cobalt blue on the shadow side, allowing the two to mix.

◀ 3 Continue adding darker paint to areas away from the light, tipping the paper to form crinkly edges. The deepest colours are alizarin crimson/bright red and alizarin crimson with a touch of ultramarine.

▶ 3 Use bright red/alizarin crimson for the front petal. Paint back blossoms and buds with a pale wash of the mixture used in step 1. Wash out some parts of the front petal and add strong cadmium yellow to the flower centre.

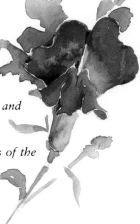

Red

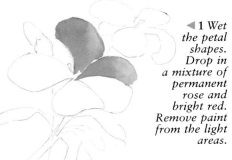

◀ **1** Wet the petal shapes. Drop in a mixture of permanent rose and bright red. Remove paint from the light areas.

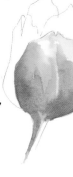

▶ **1** Damp each petal in turn and drop in cadmium yellow and cadmium red. Let it pool towards the bottom of the flower. Add a touch of sap green as it dries.

Geranium

SIMPLE STAR

▶ **2** Paint a stronger mixture into the nearer petals. Use very dilute paint for the far blossom.

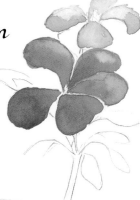

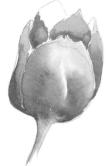

◀ **2** Fill in further petals as before. Add a touch of alizarin crimson to the petal shadows.

Tulip

BOWL

◀ **3** Strengthen the shadows and petal veins with full strength mixture. Add a touch of cobalt blue to the lower petal tips.

▶ **3** Use full strength paint in various colours for petal details.

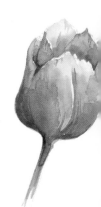

1 *Paint upper petals in permanent rose. Leave highlights to indicate the shiny surface.*

◀ **1** *Paint dilute cadmium yellow where the light hits the petal tops. Drop in bright red while it is still wet.*

Poinsettia

MULTIHEADED

Fuchsia

TRUMPET

2 *Add bright red to the darker areas and a strong mixture of the two for petal shadows. Wash violet alizarin onto lower petals. Drop in hint of permanent rose.*

▶ **2** *Build up the other petals with full strength bright red. Add a touch of brown madder where petals overlap.*

▼ **3** *Wet each central brace and drop in cadmium yellow, bright red and sap green. Paint deeper washes of bright red and brown madder on the petals farthest from the light. Paint veins on a few to sharpen them.*

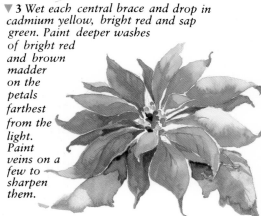

▶ **3** *Reinforce flower details with appropriate colours.*

ORIENTAL POPPIES

Shirley Trevena
(21" × 28")

POPPIES HAVE THE quality of crumpled silk, crisp and papery. Petal shadows tend to be a mass of tiny triangles and lozenges of tone, and petal edges are serrated and jagged. This painting captures the colour and vibrancy of a mass of overblown blooms. Colours range from permanent rose, through bright red and deep madder to alizarin crimson and are painted wet in wet.

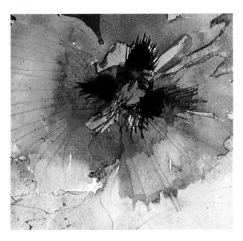

▼ *The unpredictable patterns that result when wet paint is dropped into drying paint have been utilized here to create frilled petals.*

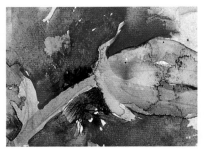

▲ *The radiating petals of this full-face poppy are emphasized with lines scratched into the paper with a twig. Dark paint settles and soft washes of colour are allowed to blend on top.*

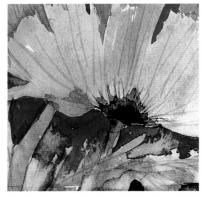

◄ *The distinctive shape of this poppy is created by the coloured areas surrounding it, and its translucency enhanced by their intensity of tone. The focal point is the junction of stem to flower.*

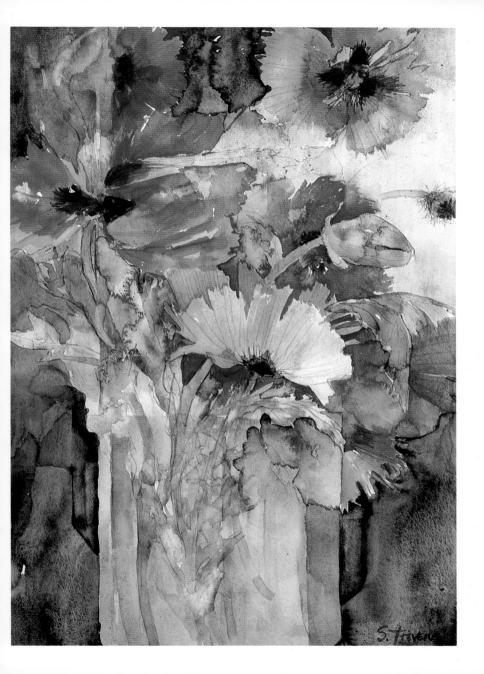

Pink

Foxglove

BELL

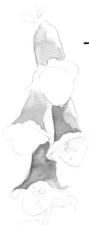

◀ **1** *Paint a light wash of permanent rose, leaving white highlights. Add a second wash of magenta and a pale shadow of cobalt blue/ permanent rose inside the flowers.*

▶ **2** *Add further washes to build up the shape. Pick out the inside bell pattern with a magenta/ sap green mix.*

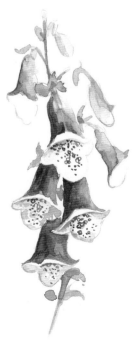

▶ **1** *Wash the sun-facing petals with lemon yellow. Leaving some areas clear, wash permanent rose/lemon yellow onto mid-tone petals. Tip the paper to let it flow into deep areas.*

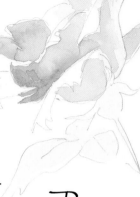

Rose

BOWL

2 *Add cobalt blue for darker petals. Use ultramarine and alizarin crimson with the mix for the darkest petals.*

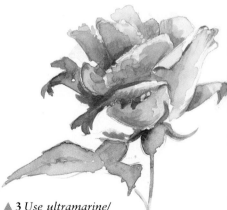

▲ **3** *Use ultramarine/ alizarin to mould petals and dry paint for petal lines and points. Add a touch of cobalt blue to the bowl of the flower. Sap green/ cobalt blue for leaves.*

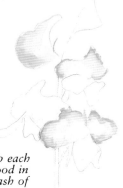

► **1** *Paint a pale wash of cadmium yellow onto back petals. Use a watery mix of lemon yellow and permanent rose on the front petal.*

►**1** *Damp each petal. Flood in a pale wash of permanent rose/lemon yellow. Push it to the edges of the petals. Dab out the centres.*

Sweet pea

LIPPED

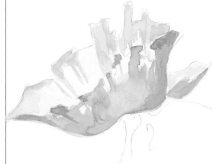

◄**2** *Add more of the same mix as it dries brushing the paint to make petal ruffles. Add a light wash of the mix to the back petals.*

Oriental poppy

BOWL

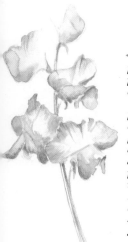

◄**2** *Add further petals as before. Use a fine brush for details and petal ruffles. Paint leaves sap green.*

► **3** *Use the mix fairly dry to pick out petal folds and shadows. Paint the flower centre with cadmium yellow/alizarin violet. Build up leaves with washes of sap green. Make these darker nearer the flower, to define its shape.*

Pink

▶1 *Paint a variegated wash of lemon yellow on sun-facing petals.*

Gerbera

RAY

▶2 *Use rose dore for a second wash. Allow it to settle in shadowed areas.*

◀3 *Paint a little permanent rose onto some petals. Add burnt umber to permanent rose for shadows. Mix alizarin violet with burnt umber for flower centre. Paint spikes of strong Indian yellow around it.*

◀1 *Mask stamens. Working each floret separately, lay a pale wash of permanent rose.*

Nerene

MULTIHEADED

▶2 *Paint a darker wash on the nearer petals and add cobalt blue for shadow.*

▲3 *Build up a flower head from the separate florets using the same colours paler for the distant blooms. Remove masking. Add dark cadmium yellow florets. Sap green for stem.*

Pink

SIMPLE STAR

▶ **1** *Paint a wash of rose dore/ cadmium yellow. Make it darker at the petal edges. Leave white highlights.*

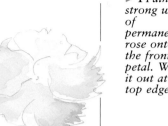

2 *Damp each petal in turn and paint a wash of permanent rose. Drop stronger paint onto petal edges and shadows.*

▶ **3** *Add alizarin crimson to the rose mix. Reinforce the petal edges by washing paint into the tips. Use shades of the colours to paint petal lines and markings. Add a cobalt green centre.*

▶ **1** *Paint a strong wash of permanent rose onto the front petal. Wash it out at the top edges.*

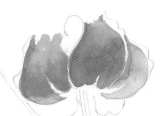

Lily

TRUMPET

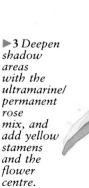

◀ **2** *Mix a little ultramarine and paint the deeper petals.*

▶ **3** *Deepen shadow areas with the ultramarine/ permanent rose mix, and add yellow stamens and the flower centre.*

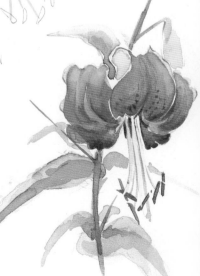

Pink

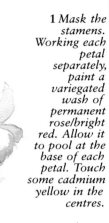

1 *Mask the stamens. Working each petal separately, paint a variegated wash of permanent rose/bright red. Allow it to pool at the base of each petal. Touch some cadmium yellow in the centres.*

Gladioli
SPIKE

▲ **2** *Using a stronger mixture, work the darker petals. Add some cobalt blue for the distant petals.*

► **3** *Use strong paint to paint petal ridges. Remove masking fluid and add sap green to the flower centres. Mix with phthalo green for leaves.*

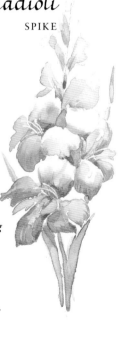

◄ **1** *Paint a variegated wash of permanent rose, dropping in some Naples yellow on the upper and sun-facing petals.*

► **2** *Use stronger permanent rose for a second wash and add some cobalt violet to lower petals. Paint central disc lemon yellow. Drop in some brown pink.*

Aster
RAY

◄ **3** *Sharpen and define some petals with strong colour. Cobalt green for leaves.*

Rhododendron

MULTIHEADED

Cyclamen

TRUMPET

▲ **1** *Build up petals with light washes of permanent rose. Leave light areas white.*

2 *Add a touch of cobalt blue for darker parts. Lightly paint a wash of cobalt green on leaf.*

▼ **3** *Use sap green for dark pattern on leaf. Add rose dore for stem. Use strong rose dore for petal pattern.*

▶ **1** *Paint a pale wash of cadmium yellow into the sun-facing petals. Put deeper colour in the centres. Mask the stamens with masking fluid.*

2 *Damp each petal in turn. Touch dry permanent rose onto the edges.*

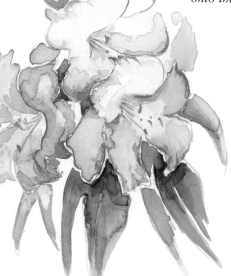

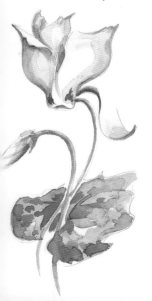

▲ **3** *Paint darker petals in permanent rose. Add a trace of magenta for petal shadows and cobalt blue for the darkest areas. Use raw sienna/cadmium yellow for stamens, and sap green for leaves.*

April Bouquet with Bowl

William C. Wright
(28" × 21")

FABRIC AND FLOWERS successfully combine to create a rainbow of colours and a patchwork of pattern. Such busyness could become distressing to the eye but here the artist uses a subtle web of line, stem and leaf to draw the viewer into the focal point of the painting. Strong yellows, reds, pinks and purples are arranged symmetrically, interspersed with white lilies and dark foliage.

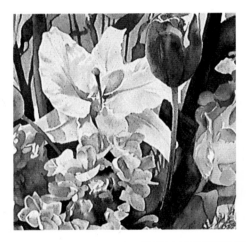

▼ *Purple is a very dense colour which tends to recede. This tulip is painted in a whole range of shades from pink to indigo/violet.*

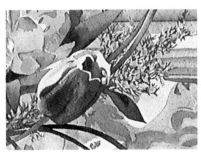

▲ *Cool blue grey describes the shadow and frilled edges of the lily petals. Trumpet-shaped flowers often have strong central spines to their petals which lead to the heart of the flower. Pools of shadow on the lilac emphasize its waxy character.*

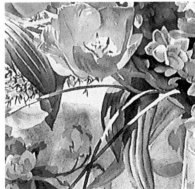

◄ *Flowers set on a light surface will catch some reflected light. The shaded petals of this tulip are a deep rich red but touched with paler colour at the base.*

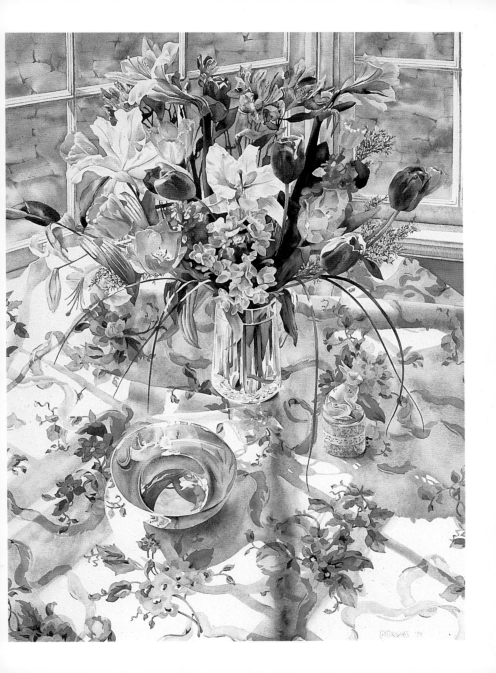

Purple

Lavender

Passion Flower

RAY

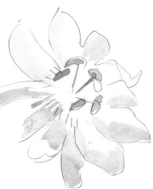

▶**1** *Wash soft cobalt blue/ permanent rose into darker areas of the petals. Paint the stamens in strong lemon yellow with touches of sap green.*

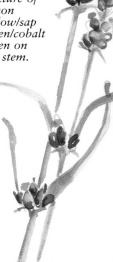

◀**1** *Paint each floret separately in ultramarine/ permanent mauve. Drop water in to push the colour into hard edges.*

2 *Work darker areas with a stronger mix. Use a pinker shade for the rays.*

▶**2** *Add further florets with tiny mauve flowers on some. Use a mixture of lemon yellow/sap green/cobalt green on the stem.*

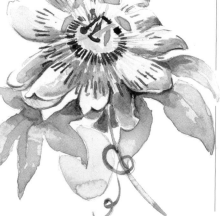

▶**3** *Add the fine details in lemon yellow, strong permanent rose and alizarin crimson. Also add a touch of this to the edges of the leaves prior to a loose wash.*

Thistle

MULTIHEADED

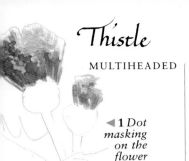

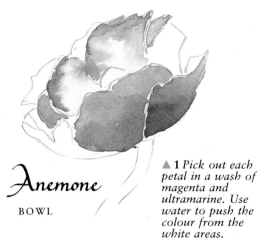

◄ 1 Dot masking on the flower head to create

highlights. Wash cobalt violet over the whole shape. Add more as it dries, and touches of permanent mauve.

2 Create the shadows with stong alizarin violet and allow them to flow into the bulbous shape below.

▼ 3 Rub off the masking fluid. Using a very fine brush paint the spikes with strong alizarin violet. Use the same brush for prickles in the cobalt green foliage.

Anemone

BOWL

▲ 1 Pick out each petal in a wash of magenta and ultramarine. Use water to push the colour from the white areas.

2 Add more ultramarine and work the darker areas. Leave a fine line round each petal to highlight the slightly shaggy edge.

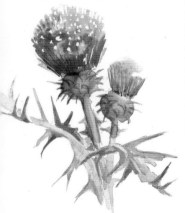

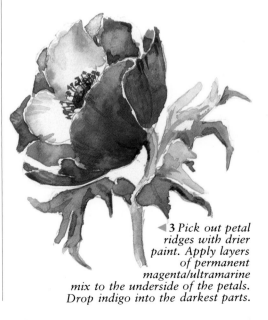

◄ 3 Pick out petal ridges with drier paint. Apply layers of permanent magenta/ultramarine mix to the underside of the petals. Drop indigo into the darkest parts.

Purple

Pansy

LIPPED

▶ **1**
Leaving
a space
for the
yellow
apron,
drop
in fairly
wet alizarin
violet. Mix
with a touch
of ultramarine for
the front petal.

2 Work stronger paint into the
petals, and a mix of
ultramarine/permanent rose for
top petals.

▲ **3** With a
fine brush
and dry paint
fill in
the central
shape in
cadmium yellow and
strong alizarin violet.

Aster

SIMPLE STAR

▶ **1** Paint
each petal
with dilute cobalt
violet/ultramarine.
Allow it to pool at the
tip of each petal.

◀ **2** Pick
out the
back petals
and
shadowed
areas in a
stronger
mix. Paint
the flower
centres in
lemon
yellow, with
cadmium
yellow
dropped in
as it dries.

▶ **3**
Add more
ultramarine
and pick out
deeper
shadows and
tiny triangle
shapes
round the
yellow
dome. Drop
wet dots of
brown pink
into its
darker side.

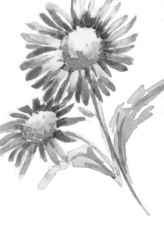

Fritillary

BELL

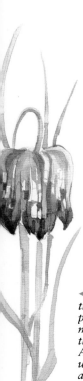

◀ **1** Build the basic bell shape with a delicate wash of alizarin crimson/ultramarine.

2 Overlay washes of the same colour with cadmium red to vary colour and create depth. Leave white areas of patterning.

◀ **3** Build up the shape and pattern using mixes of the three colours. Add details with dry paint and a fine brush. Leaves and stem in cobalt blue/sap green wash.

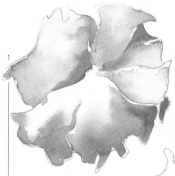

◀ **1** Paint each area with a loose wash of permanent mauve, leaving the upper areas almost white and adding the faintest touch of lemon yellow. Work alizarin violet into the shadows as it dries.

▶ **2** Shape the ruffled petals with deeper washes and patches of both colours.

Petunia

TRUMPET

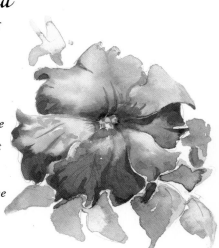

▶ **3** Add ultramarine to the mix to pick out the deep trumpet and the veins on the petals.

DAISIES AND CORNFLOWERS

Elisabeth Harden
(14" × 18")

THIS PAINTING CAPTURES the ragged nature of cornflowers and the fresh vitality of daisies. It is painted with a cool palette, basically ultramarine, cobalt and indigo blues enlivened with touches of yellow for the daisy centres and a raw sienna wash for the background. The thrusting and winding stems have been suggested by painting layers of shadow around them. The distant flowers are painted with just a hint of shape and colour, while foreground flowers have been emphasized with detail.

▼ *Ultramarine has been used for these cornflowers, full strength for the closer flower heads and very dilute for the background. Masking fluid was initially used to protect the shapes of the stamens.*

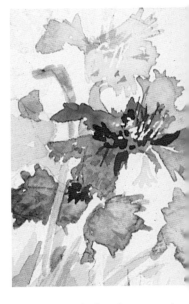

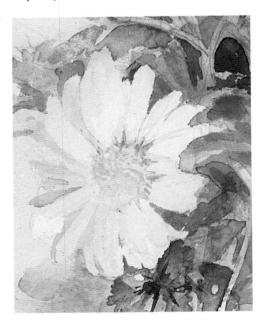

▲ *Painting a dark colour round a white flower will create a solid form. The shape is built up by adding a flower centre, shadow and sharp triangles of detail. Treat petals as blocks of tone rather than individually.*

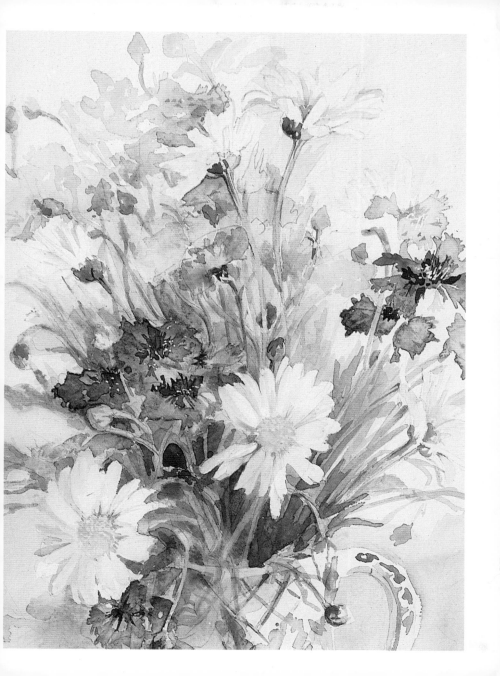

Blue

1 *Mask stamens. Flood the petal shapes with ultramarine. Remove it from the upper petals as it dries.*

Cornflower

RAY

▲ **2** *Build up the centre with cobalt violet adding alizarin crimson stamens.*

▶ **3** *Remove masking fluid. Emphasise florets with stronger ultramarine. Use cobalt green/ lemon yellow mix for leaves.*

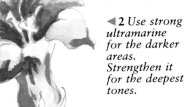

▶ **1** *Establish the mid-toned petals with a variegated wash of phthalo blue. As it dries touch in specks of permanent rose.*

◀ **2** *Use strong ultramarine for the darker areas. Strengthen it for the deepest tones.*

Gentian

TRUMPET

▶ **3** *Build up the trumpet with ridges of paint. Add crisp edges. Paint leaves with cadmium yellow/sap green.*

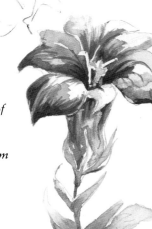

Delphinium

SPIKE

▼ **1** Dampen the flower shapes and drop in cobalt violet, ultramarine, ultramarine/ phthalo blue and alizarin violet. Allow the colours to blend slightly and drop in more as they dry.

Scabious

RAY

◀ **1** Mask stamens. Paint a delicate wash of cobalt blue/ permanent rose. Drop in water to push paint to the petal edges.

◀ **2** Add a darker wash to deeper-toned areas and shadow. Dot a pinker mix into the central dome and surround with cobalt green.

▶ **3** Remove masking. Use various cadmium yellow/cobalt green/phthalo blue mixes for leaves and buds.

▶ **2** Use stronger paint and a fine brush

to build up the flower shapes, retaining the haze of blues. Sap green for leaves.

Blue

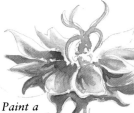

▶ **1** *Paint a
pale wash of
cerulean blue,
leaving petal
ridges white.
Add lemon
yellow and
paint the
curling anthers.
Paint darker
petals with
cerulean/
ultramarine mix.*

Blue Poppy

BOWL

▲ **1** *Paint a
light wash
of phthalo
blue into
each petal,
leaving
white
highlights.*

2 *Add more phthalo
blue and paint into
some of the darker
areas, pulling the
paint into petal
ridges.*

Love-in-the-mis

R A

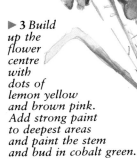

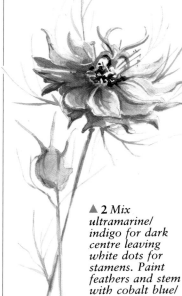

▶ **3** *Build
up the
flower
centre
with
dots of
lemon yellow
and brown pink.
Add strong paint
to deepest areas
and paint the stem
and bud in cobalt green.*

▲ **2** *Mix
ultramarine/
indigo for dark
centre leaving
white dots for
stamens. Paint
feathers and stem
with cobalt blue/
lemon yellow
mix.*

Geranium
SIMPLE STAR

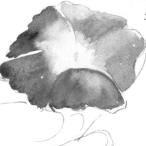

▶ **1** *Dampen each petal. Paint an ultramarine wash, leaving the flower centre white. Add a little alizarin violet to the upper petals.*

Morning glory
TRUMPET

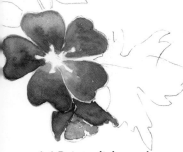

▲ **1** *Paint a light wash of permanent rose/ultramarine. Add more paint as it dries to create an uneven effect. Paint a second wash of ultramarine and build up the lower flower with petal shapes of watery paint.*

▲ **2** *Paint a second wash of stronger ultramarine/alizarin violet. Darken the paint towards the edges. Mask the stigma. Paint flower centre Indian yellow.*

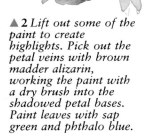

▲ **2** *Lift out some of the paint to create highlights. Pick out the petal veins with brown madder alizarin, working the paint with a dry brush into the shadowed petal bases. Paint leaves with sap green and phthalo blue.*

▶ **3** *Use stronger paint to indicate petal flow and uneven edges. Paint two washes of sap green for leaves. Add alizarin violet for winding stems.*

Blue

LIPPED

▶**1** *Use cerulean blue for lighter, distant flowers, and cobalt blue for closer, brighter flowers. Drop dots of paint to create flower heads. Allow some of the dots to blend and add touches of permanent rose.*

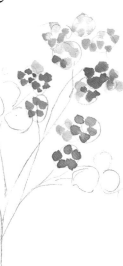

◀**1** *Damp the top petal and paint a veil of lemon yellow. Add cobalt blue to lower edges. Feed in more paint as it dries. Build up other petals in the same way. Paint bright lemon yellow anthers with touches of brown pink.*

Forget-me-not

MULTIHEADED

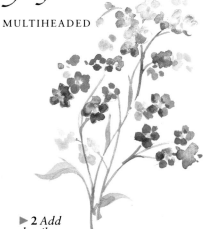

◀**2** *Add a little violet and paint the lower petals, leaving the apron white.*

▶**3** *Paint more layers. Use strong alizarin violet for deep shadows and petal markings.*

▶**2** *Add detail to some close flowers. Use cadmium yellow for a few flower centres. Link all flowers with threads of stems of sap green.*

◀ **1** *Paint the shapes of the flowers with a mix of ultramarine and permanent rose. As it dries add more ultramarine to the shadowed side.*

▶ **1** *Paint a loose wash using ultramarine/ rose madder for the upper petals and phthalo blue for the shadowed parts. Drop in lemon yellow as it dries.*

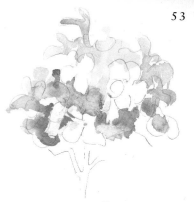

Hydrangea

MULTIHEADED

Bluebell

TRUMPET

◀ **2** *Paint a second wash, giving definition to deep-set areas and particular petals.*

▶ **2** *Add definition with a deeper mix and paint the undersides of flowers with a pale pink mix. Add leaves with washes of sap green.*

▶ **3** *Using the same colours build up a mass of florets. Mix lemon yellow and phthalo blue for the leaves.*

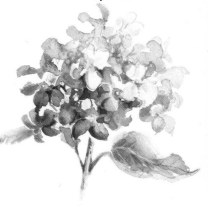

WHITE ROSES

Elisabeth Harden
(5½" × 5½")

FLOWERS PAINTED CLOSE up develop a different dimension, areas of shadow become a landscape in themselves, and subtle gradations of colour create hills and valleys. A limited palette has been used – phthalo green, cobalt green, indigo, cadmium yellow and brown pink, giving the painting a monochromatic feel. The artist pushed the paint into hard edges with a brush and hairdryer to create the frilled petals.

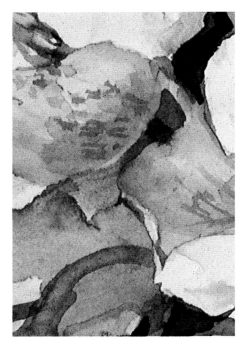

▼ *The anthers were masked and painted in a mixture of colours. They are a focal point of the picture.*

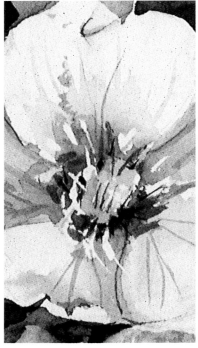

▲ *The dark phthalo green/indigo mix used for the background was gently brushed onto each petal making sure that the area under the overlapping petal edge was darkest.*

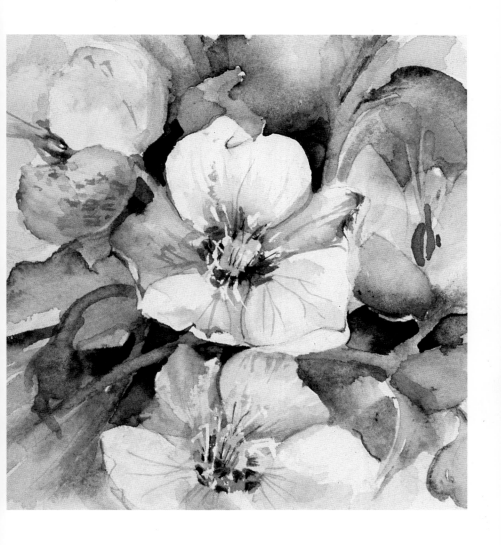

White and cream

Lily
TRUMPET

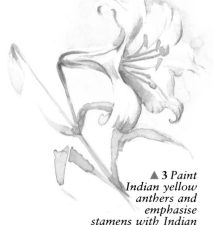

◀ **1** Outline
the flower
with Naples
yellow/cobalt blue mix.
Paint shadows with
cobalt blue.

2 Use permanent rose for ridges
on trumpet and underside of
petals. Add touches of rose and
cobalt for petal ridges and frills.
Use strong lemon yellow
for flower centre.

▲ **3** Paint
Indian yellow
anthers and
emphasise
stamens with Indian
yellow/cobalt blue mix.

Snowdrop
BELL

▶ **1** Use
ultramarine
wash to define
each flower
shape. Push
colour towards
edges to sharpen
some outlines.

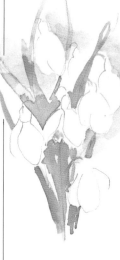

◀ **2** Paint a wash
of phthalo blue
and lemon yellow
to make a block
of leaf shapes.
Use same darker
wash for lower
stems and cobalt
blue/lemon
yellow for petal
pattern.

▶ **3** Paint
flower stems
and sepals in
cobalt blue/
lemon yellow.
Add
ultramarine/
lemon yellow
to clarify leaf
shapes. For
petals use a
touch of
indigo.

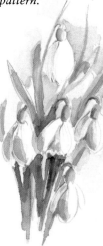

Apple blossom

SIMPLE STAR

Water lily

BOWL

▶ **1** For the shadow of upper petals use cobalt blue, adding a trace of brown pink. Use a deeper mixture for the lower petals.

▲ **1** Use a loose wash of cadmium yellow/sap green for the blossom outlines. Paint patches of dilute permanent rose for mid-tone petal areas, leaving large areas of white.

◀ **2** Paint deeper shadows in cobalt blue. Stamens in lemon and Indian yellow. Indian yellow/sap green wash on leaves.

2 Paint a darker wash on the leaves. Blend some of the green paint into the pink for shadows.

▼ **3** Use stronger mixes of flower and leaf colours to build up depth and colour, and fine brushwork for stamens and deepest crevices.

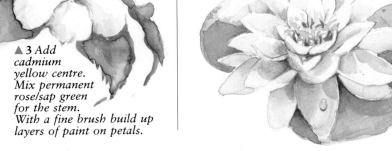

▲ **3** Add cadmium yellow centre. Mix permanent rose/sap green for the stem. With a fine brush build up layers of paint on petals.

White and cream

▶ **1** *Paint a variegated wash of ultramarine around the flower. Use dark areas to emphasise the whitest petals.*

▲ **1** *Outline the white petals with a pale cobalt blue/lemon yellow mix. Use strong lemon yellow for each flower centre.*

Daisy

RAY

Cape Primrose

TRUMPET

2 *For shadows on petals use cobalt blue, dropping in some Indian yellow. For back petals and deep shadows use ultramarine with traces of alizarin crimson, use lemon for the dome.*

2 *To build up the trumpet shapes gradually add touches of cobalt blue.*

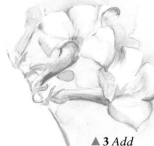

◀ **3** *Moisten the dome. Build the shadowed side with drops of Indian yellow and brown pink. Pick out crevices with ultramarine.*

▲ **3** *Add phthalo blue for the darkest shadows and hints of definition on petals.*

◄ 1 *Paint a light lemon yellow wash on the petals, leaving plenty of white. Use strong Indian yellow for flower centres.*

Rose

BOWL

Frangipani

TRUMPET

1 *Paint a wash of Naples/lemon yellow onto the petals. Leave white highlights.*

▲ 2 *Surround the flower with a wash of sap green/rose dore. Paint darker areas of petals with Naples/lemon yellows.*

◄ 2 *Establish flower shape with a wash of lemon yellow/sap green. Use pale cobalt blue for shadows and alizarin violet for deeper shadows.*

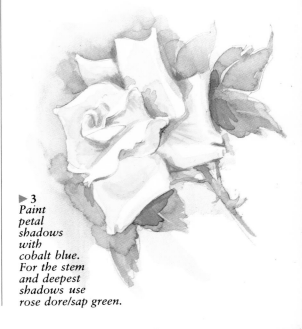

◄ 3 *Work into leaves with darker sap green. Sharpen flower centre and underside of stems with brown pink emphasising whirly character of blossom.*

► 3 *Paint petal shadows with cobalt blue. For the stem and deepest shadows use rose dore/sap green.*

Green

1 *Paint a pale wash of lemon yellow on each petal. Then a second wash of lemon/ cobalt blue. Use tissue to dab out highlights.*

▶ **1** Establish the flower outline with a cadmium yellow/ sap green wash, pushing it towards the edges. Paint the inside of the trumpet with cobalt blue/sap green mix. Tip the paper so that the paint pools in deepest shadow areas.

▶ **2** Moisten the apron and paint the frill in alizarin crimson so that colour pools at edges. Add fine crimson lines on petals.

Easter lily
TRUMPET

Orchid
LIPPED

▲ **2** *Add touches of indigo for underside of petals. Paint stamen in strong cadmium yellow.*

▶ **3** *Use appropriate colours to build up tone and fine details.*

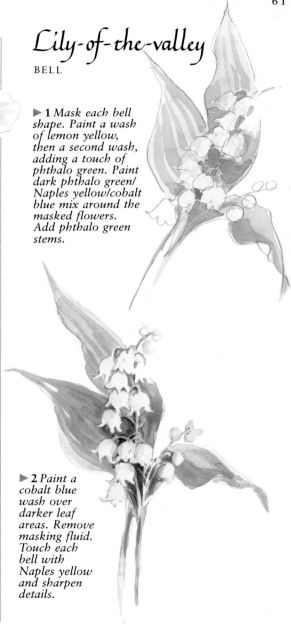

►**1** *Make tiny stars with masking fluid for lightest florets. Paint a wash of lemon yellow.*

Lady's mantle

MULTIHEADED

2 *Add masking fluid. For the second wash add cobalt blue.*

◄ **3** *Add more cobalt and paint the top leaves. Add a little phthalo blue and paint darker leaves and shadows. Leave fine lines to pick out serrated edges.*

Lily-of-the-valley

BELL

► **1** *Mask each bell shape. Paint a wash of lemon yellow, then a second wash, adding a touch of phthalo green. Paint dark phthalo green/ Naples yellow/cobalt blue mix around the masked flowers. Add phthalo green stems.*

► **2** *Paint a cobalt blue wash over darker leaf areas. Remove masking fluid. Touch each bell with Naples yellow and sharpen details.*

Leaves

Poppy

▼ **1** *Paint a light wash of lemon yellow. As it dries add a lemon yellow/cobalt green mix.*

Ivy

◀ **1** *Paint a wash of lemon yellow.*

▲ **2** *Use sap green for a second wash, omitting the leaf ribs.*

▲ **2** *Build up the leaves with patches of cobalt green. Add cobalt blue for darker touches. Emphasise petal edges with a fine brush.*

▼ **3** *Add phthalo blue and a touch of ultramarine to the mix. Paint darker patches, blending the paint with a dry brush.*

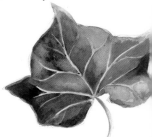

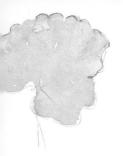

1 *Paint a wash of lemon yellow. Dab out highlights with tissue.*

▲ **1** *Paint a wash of cadmium yellow / cobalt blue. Touch in a scalloped edge with cadmium red.*

Geranium

Myrtle

▲ **2** *Mix sap green and lemon yellow. Paint a second wash, omitting leaf spines.*

▶ **2** *Add phthalo blue to the mix and paint a variegated wash.*

▼ **3** *Add cadmium red and stipple in patterning with a stiff brush.*

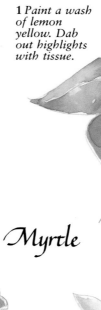

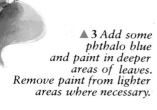

▲ **3** *Add some phthalo blue and paint in deeper areas of leaves. Remove paint from lighter areas where necessary.*

CREDITS

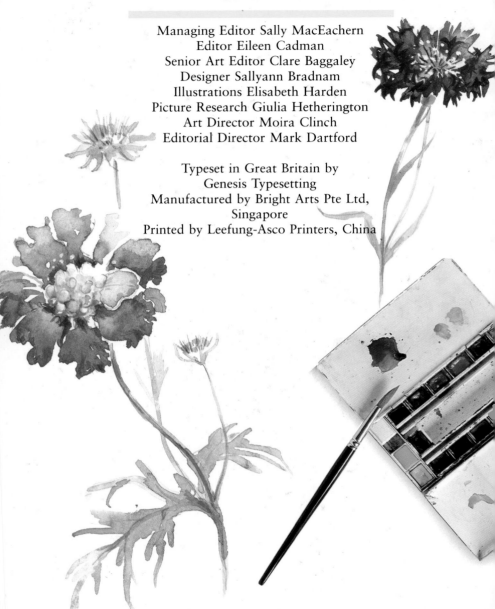

Managing Editor Sally MacEachern
Editor Eileen Cadman
Senior Art Editor Clare Baggaley
Designer Sallyann Bradnam
Illustrations Elisabeth Harden
Picture Research Giulia Hetherington
Art Director Moira Clinch
Editorial Director Mark Dartford

Typeset in Great Britain by
Genesis Typesetting
Manufactured by Bright Arts Pte Ltd,
Singapore
Printed by Leefung-Asco Printers, China